GREEK AND ROMAN MYTHS

WEBSTER EVERYREADERS

GREEK
and
ROMAN MYTHS

Edited by   **WILLIAM KOTTMEYER**
St. Louis Public Schools

Adapted by   **KAY WARE**
St. Louis Public Schools

and   **LUCILLE SUTHERLAND**
St. Louis Public Schools

Illustrated by **EDWARD MILLER**

WEBSTER DIVISION, McGRAW-HILL BOOK COMPANY
St. Louis • New York • San Francisco • Dallas • Toronto • London

The Webster Everyreaders

Th e EVERYREADERS were selected from the great literature of the world and adapted to the needs of today's children. This series retains the flavor of the originals, providing mature content and dramatic plot structure, along with eye appeal designed to motivate reading.

This approach was first developed in the renowned St. Louis Reading Clinic by Dr. Kottmeyer and is the direct outgrowth of wide and successful teaching of remedial reading.

A high interest level plus the carefully controlled vocabulary and sentence structure enable pupils to read the stories easily, confidently, and with enjoyment.

Twelfth Printing, 1972.

ISBN 07-033738-1

CONTENTS

The GREEK *and* ROMAN GODS

We remember the old Greeks and Romans for many reasons. The Greeks and Romans built beautiful buildings many, many years ago. The Greeks were great artists and writers. The Romans were mighty soldiers and famous lawmakers. We still study the work of these great people.

Of course we know many things today which the old Greeks did not know. We know much more about science than they did. They did not know how big the world is. They knew only a small part of the world. They did not know what caused the sun to rise and set. They did not know much about the moon and stars and planets.

But they were good story tellers. They made up stories to explain what they saw. They believed that there were many gods. Each god had his own work to do. So they had a god of war, a god of harvests, a god of the sun. There were gods of the skies, of the earth, of the sea, of the underworld. They believed the gods lived on Mount Olympus. Here they met to eat and drink. Here, too, many had their palaces.

The people believed the gods were strong and wise. When earth people did things to please the gods, the gods helped them. They might make crops grow better. They might give a man great riches. They might help him in war. When the gods were angry, they punished people. They might kill a man or change him into an animal or plant. They might send storms or floods.

Sometimes the gods did not get along very well. They were sometimes angry and jealous of one another. Sometimes they fought.

Jupiter was king of the gods. He was the

2

wisest and strongest of all. When he was angry he threw his thunder and lightning across the skies. Then the earth shook and the people hid. The other gods would stay out of his path when he was angry.

Juno was Jupiter's wife and queen of the gods. Juno was beautiful, but was very jealous. She often got angry with Jupiter, but she knew he was stronger than she.

The Greeks believed that Apollo was the sun god. They said he drove a flaming chariot across the sky each day. Apollo's chariot was the sun.

Mercury was the messenger of the gods. He wore a cap and shoes with wings. The wings carried him swiftly from one end of the earth to the other. We still use Mercury's name today in many ways.

Another god was Vulcan, who made spears and shields and armor. He had a work shop underground. Great fires burned in his dark caves. Vulcan made things for the gods and people of the earth.

There were many other gods. Venus was the goddess of love and beauty. Neptune was god of the sea. Most of the gods were the same for both the Greeks and the Romans. Jupiter is the Roman name for the king of the gods. The Greeks called him Zeus. The Greek name for Juno is Hera. Each god has both a Greek name and a Roman name. In these stories the Roman names are used because they are usually shorter and easier.

Nobody believes in these gods any more, but we still like to read the stories about them. These stories have been told for thousands of years. They are full of wonders and adventures, so even if we do not believe them, we can still enjoy the stories.

PROMETHEUS

Jupiter was king of the gods. Usually the gods and goddesses did what he told them to do. But once a god did not obey Jupiter. His name was Prometheus. This is his story.

Prometheus was very much interested in the earth. He loved its people. Often he sat on Mt. Olympus and watched them. When winter came he saw that they were unhappy. The people had no way to keep warm. Prometheus did not like to see them suffer.

"What can I do to help them?" he said. "Jupiter will not let man have fire. If something isn't done they will die. I know.

I'll go ask Vulcan to see if he will help."

Vulcan was the blacksmith of the gods. He lived deep under the earth. Vulcan had great fires burning in his shop. "Maybe," thought Prometheus, "I can get some fire from him. Then I will take it to the earth. It will keep the poor people warm. I'll go see Vulcan no matter what Jupiter says."

Down to the earth he went. When he came to a great cave, he stopped. Dark slippery steps went down inside the cave. Carefully he went down.

After a while he saw a light. It came from under a door. Inside he heard hammering and pounding. Knocking on the door he called, "Vulcan, open the door. It's Prometheus." The hammering stopped. The door opened. Vulcan, wearing a leather apron, stood before him.

"What do you want here, Prometheus? You are a long way from Olympus. Can I do something for you?"

"I came to ask a favor. The people on earth are my friends. It is winter there. They have no heat. They will freeze to

death if they don't get help. I know that fire belongs only to the gods. They will not give it to anyone else. That's why I came to you. Can I take some fire from your shop? No one will know."

"I cannot give you the fire, Prometheus. You know that. But why don't you stay awhile? You can look around. I must get back to work."

He winked at Prometheus. Turning his back, he went to work. Prometheus knew what he meant. Vulcan would say nothing if Prometheus took some fire. But he could not give it to him.

That was all the god needed. He took a piece of heavy wood. He held it in the flame. It caught fire quickly.

As soon as it was burning, he opened the door. Turning, he whispered, "Thanks, Vulcan. You are a good friend." He ran quickly up the steps.

He showed his friends on earth how to use the fire. They built fires to keep warm. They learned to cook their food. Wild animals were frightened away. The people on earth were happy with the fire. They were very thankful to Prometheus.

Prometheus was happy, too. But not for long. Jupiter soon saw the fires burning on the earth. He was very angry.

"Only the gods have fire!" he shouted. "It is not for people on earth. How did they get fire? Who gave it to them?"

No one would tell. Each of the gods was asked about it. No one knew who had given the fire.

"I'll find out for myself," roared Jupiter.

He rushed down to the earth. Straight to Vulcan he went. Breaking through the door he shouted, "Did you give those people fire? If you did I shall punish you!"

Vulcan did not want to tell. He did not answer.

"I want an answer! Who gave those people fire?"

No one could say no to Jupiter when he talked like that. Vulcan had to answer. "It was Prometheus," he said.

"So — it was Prometheus! He will pay for this. You, Vulcan, must do as I tell you. Make some heavy chains. I will chain Prometheus to a lonely rock. There he will stay. He must be punished."

Vulcan did not want to make the chains. But Jupiter was the king of the gods. Everyone obeyed him. The chains were made. Vulcan dragged them to the rock.

Jupiter already had Prometheus waiting there.

"I am sorry, Prometheus," said Vulcan sadly. "I do not like to do this. But Jupiter is very angry. He wants to see you punished."

He fastened the chains on the god's arms and legs. One end of the chain he drove into the rock. Prometheus could move only a few feet.

Fierce hungry birds came flying around him. They pecked at his eyes, and bit him. He could not beat them off. Year after year passed, and Prometheus still sat on the lonely rock. He gave up hope of ever being free again.

Now there lived in Greece a mighty man named Hercules. No one had ever seen a man so strong as he. Once his king sent him to another country. On the way he passed the rock where Prometheus was chained. Just then an eagle was clawing Prometheus.

"What a terrible thing!" said Hercules. "The man is chained. He cannot help himself."

He raised his bow and let an arrow fly. The poisoned arrow struck the eagle's heart. With a scream it fell into the sea. Hercules climbed the rock.

"My name is Hercules," he said. "I am going to break those chains for you."

One twist of his mighty arms and Prometheus was free.

"I do not know how to thank you!" cried Prometheus. "I have sat on this lonely rock for years. I thought nobody would ever help me. Can I do something for you? I would do anything to pay you back."

"Yes, Prometheus," said Hercules, "you can help me. You can help me very much."

And Prometheus did help him.

ATLAS

Many years ago, the first book of maps had a picture of a man holding up the world. The man's name was Atlas. People began calling it "the Atlas book." Later they just called it an "Atlas." Now, after many years, the name Atlas has come to mean a book of maps. This old Greek story tells about Atlas.

Hercules was one of the Greek heroes. He was the strong man who broke the chains for Prometheus. Prometheus was very thankful for what he had done.

"You saved my life, Hercules. Is there anything I can do to pay you back? I would like to do something for you."

"Yes, Prometheus, there is something you can do. My king gave me a job. He sent me to find some golden apples. I have no idea where to look for them. You are wise. Do you know where they are?"

"I've heard of those apples, Hercules. They are in the garden of the Hesperides. These Hesperides are young women. I'm not sure where to find them or their garden. But I can tell you where to find their father. His name is Atlas."

Hercules was pleased and excited.

"Tell me where I can find Atlas. I'll start now to look for him."

"It's not as easy as all that, Hercules. First you must go to the edge of the world. That is the place where the world ends. When you reach that place, you will find Atlas. Look over the edge of the world. You will see a giant. He holds the whole world on his shoulders. That is Atlas."

"I'll find him, Prometheus. What do I ask Atlas when I see him?"

"He is the father of the young women.

He knows where to find them. He might tell you where they are. Maybe he will get the apples for you."

Hercules started out to find Atlas.

"If I follow a straight line," he said, "I'll have to come to the edge of the world sometime."

He walked in a straight line. After a long time he came to the edge of the world.

"This must be it," he thought. "There's nothing ahead. I'll look down under the edge. Atlas should be there if what Prometheus said is true."

He leaned over the edge to look. There he saw a giant. The giant's big muscles were doubled up. Sweat rolled from his face. The world rested on his shoulders.

"Are you Atlas?" Hercules called.

"Yes, I'm Atlas," panted the giant. "And I'm tired of this heavy load. Holding the world on your shoulders isn't an easy job. I'm the strongest of all men and I'm worn out. Who are you?"

"I am Hercules. Prometheus told me to find you. He said you might help me. I must get some golden apples. I don't know where to find them. Prometheus said they were in your daughters' garden. Would you tell me where that garden is?"

"You mean the garden of the Hesperides. Yes, I know where it is. I wish there were someone to hold the world for me. I'd go get the apples for you."

The real truth was that Atlas was tired. He had held the earth for years. This seemed a chance to be free for a while.

"Maybe," he thought, "I can talk Hercules into holding it." So he said, "Hercules, how strong are you?"

"I'm very strong, Atlas. I broke the chains to free Prometheus. Why do you ask?"

"I was wondering," said Atlas, "if you were strong enough to hold the world. No one except me has ever held it. If you hold it, I'll get the apples."

"I'm sure I'm strong enough to hold it, Atlas. I'll stoop down and you slide it on to my shoulders. I think I can hold it until you come back."

16

All the earth shook as Atlas and Hercules changed places. It was heavier than Hercules had thought. He drew his muscles tight. He braced his feet. He would show Atlas he was strong.

"Atlas," he said, "I'm all right now. You get the apples. But don't stay too long."

Atlas took a deep breath. He shook his shoulders. For the first time in years he was able to stand up straight.

"How happy I am to be rid of that heavy load! Now I'll go see my daughters. I'll bring the golden apples to Hercules. But I won't hurry."

He was gone a long time. Hercules grew more and more tired. His shoulders hurt. His back was sore. He began to worry.

"What if Atlas doesn't come back? I don't think I can hold the world much longer. What if I should drop it?"

There was no one to help Hercules. Somehow he held on. At last Atlas came back. Atlas was in no hurry to take back the heavy load. He liked being free.

"Hercules, you have done well," he said.

"There is no one else who could have held the world. I have brought the apples to you."

Hercules felt better as soon as he saw Atlas. Now he could give back the world. It was even more important than getting the apples.

"I thought you would never come, Atlas. My shoulders and back are so tired. You are right. Holding the world is not easy. If you will take it now, I will leave. I thank you for getting the apples."

"I'll be glad to take the apples to the king for you, Hercules," said Atlas. "Then I'll take the world when I come back. You are strong. You can hold it for a while longer."

Hercules had no idea of letting Atlas leave again. He had held the world long enough. He said to himself, "I'll trick Atlas into taking the world again." So he said to Atlas, "That's all right with me. But my shoulders are sore. I'd like to make a pad for them. You hold the world a minute while I make the pad."

Atlas laid down the apples. He stooped over. Hercules put the world back on the shoulders of Atlas. The trick had worked.

"Good-bye, Atlas," he called. "Thank you for getting the apples."

He climbed back on the earth before Atlas could answer.

Hercules took the golden apples to his king. Atlas was left to hold the world forever.

PANDORA'S BOX

The story of Pandora was a favorite of the Greeks. They thought it told how trouble and hope came to the world. They learned a lesson from Pandora, too.

Pandora was a beautiful girl. Jupiter, the king of the gods, sent her to Epimetheus. Epimetheus was Prometheus' brother. Jupiter had punished Prometheus for stealing fire. Now he had a plan to punish the people, too. Had they not taken Prometheus' gift?

Prometheus did not trust Jupiter. He warned his brother to be careful of Jupiter and not to trust the girl. Epimetheus was often lonely. He would not listen.

The first thing Pandora saw in Epimetheus' house was a big box. Almost the first thing she said to him was, "Epimetheus, what do you have in that box?"

"My dear Pandora," he answered, "that is a secret. You must not ask me about it. The box was left here for me to keep. I do not know what is in it."

"But who gave it to you?" asked Pandora.

"That's a secret, too," said Epimetheus.

"I don't like secrets," said Pandora. "I wish the old box weren't here."

"Oh, come, Pandora!" he said. "Don't think about it. I don't want you to be unhappy."

But Pandora could not forget the strange box. Every day she thought about it.

"Where did the box come from? What could be in it?" she kept saying.

"Always talking about the box!" Epimetheus said at last. "I wish you would try to talk about something else. Let's go for a walk."

"I don't want to go for a walk. You *must* tell me what is in the box!" said Pandora.

"I've told you fifty times. I don't know what's in the box. How can I tell you what's in it when I don't know?" He was getting a little angry.

"Well, then, at least you can tell me how you got it," said Pandora.

"Oh, all right! It was left at the door. A man brought it just before you came. He wore a strange coat, and his cap seemed to be made of feathers. It looked almost as if it had wings."

"Did he carry a cane?" asked Pandora.

"Yes, he did."

"Tell me about it," Pandora said eagerly. "What did it look like?"

"Well, it was very strange. It was like two snakes twisting around a stick. It was beautifully carved. At first I thought the snakes were alive."

"Oh, I know who the man was!" Pandora was excited now. "He is one of the gods. Mercury is his name. He's the god who brought me here. I'll bet the box is for me. Why, maybe it is filled with pretty dresses!"

"Maybe so," answered Epimetheus. "But he told me the box was not to be opened. Until he says so, we don't have any right to lift that lid." And he left the house without another word.

He walked down the road. If only Mercury had left the box somewhere else! The box, the box, nothing but the box! The worst of it was he was wondering about it, too.

After Epimetheus was gone, Pandora stood looking at the box.

"Why won't he listen to me?" she said. "I don't know why we can't open it. Mercury wouldn't care."

The box itself was very beautiful. It was made of dark, shining wood. Flowers and birds were carved around the sides. Carved on the top were beautiful children. One child's face seemed real. It seemed to speak to her.

"Don't be afraid, Pandora. It won't

hurt to open the box. Never mind Epimetheus. You are wiser than he. Open the box! See if you don't find something very pretty!"

Pandora walked closer to the box. She tried to lift it. It was heavy — far too heavy for her to lift. She raised one end a few inches from the floor. She let it fall. She thought she heard something move inside the box.

Then she saw the gold rope. The box was not fastened by a lock. Instead, a gold rope was tied around it. She looked at it.

"I believe I could untie the knot," she said to herself. "It wouldn't hurt to try. I could tie it up again right away. Even Epimetheus wouldn't get angry at me for that. I don't have to open the box just because I get the knot untied."

She touched the knot. She gave it a twist. As if by magic, it came loose.

Again she thought she heard a voice from the box —

"Let us out, dear Pandora. Let us out."

"What can it be?" thought Pandora. "Is

there something alive in the box? Well — I'll take just one peek."

At this moment, Epimetheus entered the house. He saw Pandora about to open the box. He could have cried out and stopped her. But he did not.

As Pandora raised the lid, the house grew dark. She paid no attention. She lifted the lid wide and looked inside. Out of the box flew Troubles of all kinds — sickness, greed, hate, and many others.

"Oh, I am stung!" cried Epimetheus.

Pandora let the lid fall. Then something stung her, too. Epimetheus and Pandora were both sorry. Never had they felt so unhappy.

The ugly things flew out the windows. They flew all over the earth. They would bother people forever. Jupiter's plan had succeeded.

But there was still one thing more in the box. Pandora and Epimetheus heard a soft tap from inside. A sweet voice spoke,

"Let me out. I am not like the Troubles. You need me. I can help you."

"Shall I lift the lid again?" asked Pandora.

"You might as well," said Epimetheus. "One more Trouble flying around won't make much difference."

This time they both lifted the lid. Out flew a lovely little creature called Hope.

"I was put into the box," she told them, "to make up for all those ugly Troubles. So long as I am here, Troubles will not seem so bad."

"We feel better already," said Epimetheus. "Will you stay with us always?"

"I will never be far from you," said Hope. "There may be times when you will think I am not around. Sometimes I will come to you when you least expect me. I will always be here when you need me."

Even though Pandora let Troubles into the world, people would have Hope to help them. And as long as people have Hope, they cannot always be unhappy.

PEGASUS, *the* HORSE *with* WINGS

Today everyone knows what flying horses look like. Pictures of them are everywhere. You see them on filling stations and on signs. The flying horse means great speed and power. The idea had its start long ago with a story the Greeks told about Pegasus, a flying horse.

There is also a group of stars named for Pegasus. The Greeks thought the sky was a great "picture book." Each group of stars was a picture of something they knew about.

Notice that four stars of Pegasus form a square. Turn the picture upside down. It is not hard to imagine that this is the back half of a horse. The square is the back half of the body. The other stars make the horse's head and its two back legs. You can see Pegasus in the sky in the fall of the year.

The old Greek stories often tell of fierce dragons which killed people. Many years ago such a great dragon lived in the little country called Lycia. This terrible animal had three heads — a lion's, a goat's, and a snake's. He breathed great streams of fire from his mouths. He roared over the land, burning houses and killing the people. The people were afraid to leave their homes. Their poor king did not know what to do.

At first brave men tried to hunt the dragon, but nobody ever came back alive. The people often found their broken spears or smashed shields. At last no one dared fight the dragon. The king sat in his castle, pale with fear.

In Lycia lived a brave young man named Bellerophon. He was strong and a great fighter. He heard about the dragon. So one day he went to see the king.

"My name is Bellerophon," he said. "I have come to kill the dragon."

The king shook his head sadly.

"The dragon has killed my best men. A man has no chance. Go home, young man. I do not want you to die."

"No," said Bellerophon bravely. "I am not afraid. I will kill the dragon or the dragon will kill me. So long as this dragon lives, our people cannot be happy."

"All right," said the king. "You are foolish but brave. I wish you the best of luck."

Bellerophon began to plan. He knew he could not kill the dragon alone. He had to have help. When you needed help you went to the gods. Bellerophon did not know how to go about it.

One night he could not sleep.

"How can I get the gods to help me?" he cried.

Suddenly the room began to light up. Stronger and stronger grew the light. Bellerophon sat up in surprise. Before him he saw a woman — a beautiful, shining woman. For a moment he said nothing.

"You must be one of the gods," he cried. "Who — who are you?"

"I am Minerva, Bellerophon. I have come to help you. Do just what I tell you. There is only one way to kill the dragon. Here, take this."

Minerva handed him a beautiful golden bridle. Bellerophon looked at her in surprise.

"What shall I do with it?" he asked. "I have no horse."

"Have you ever heard of the horse Pegasus?"

"The wonderful horse with wings?"

"Yes. You must hunt for him. You cannot catch him unless you have this bridle. If you slip it over his head he will be tame. He will help you kill the dragon."

"But how — ?"

Before Bellerophon could ask this question, Minerva was gone. The room grew dark again. Bellerophon rubbed his eyes. Could he have dreamed all this? Then he felt the bridle in his hand.

Early next morning he started out to

find the wonderful horse. He asked every one he met the same question.

"Have you seen Pegasus, the horse with wings?"

Most people laughed at him. They had not even heard of Pegasus. Many people thought Bellerophon was crazy. Day after day he went on asking the same question.

At last, tired and hopeless, he stopped to rest. A little boy came running by. He stopped to look at the stranger.

"Son," said Bellerophon, "you haven't seen a horse with wings, have you?"

"Yes, I have," said the boy. "I saw him yesterday. I was sailing my boats over there. As I looked into the water I could see the blue sky. Suddenly the horse flew by. I looked up, and there he was. Sometimes he comes down over there for a drink. Oh, he is a wonderful, beautiful horse! I tell people about him, but nobody else has seen him. Nobody will believe me."

Bellerophon was puzzled. Could the lad be right? This was the only hope he had.

"I will wait here," he said. "It may be

the boy is right and the horse will come."

Day after day he sat near the water.
Every day the little boy came to watch
with him.

One day they sat as always looking at
the clear blue water. The boy softly laid
his hand on Bellerophon's arm.

"Don't move," he said. "Do not look up.
I see the horse in the water."

Bellerophon's heart beat fast. Very slowly he raised his eyes. The boy was right!
A great white horse was sailing through the
air. His great wings carried him in smooth
circles. Closer and closer he came. He
seemed not to notice Bellerophon and the
boy. At last he landed lightly on the bank
a few feet away. Bellerophon saw that the
wings were shining silver. The horse bent
over to drink. Bellerophon knew that this
was his chance! He rose slowly and leaped
upon the horse's back. He had no time to
slip the golden bridle over the horse's
head. He wrapped his arms around the
horse's neck.

With one leap the horse was high in the

air. Down he shot, like a bullet, trying to throw his rider. He turned and twisted and kicked. He turned over and flew on his back. Bellerophon just hung on tighter.

At last Bellerophon saw his chance. He succeeded in slipping the bit between the horse's teeth. As soon as he did, the horse stopped fighting. Minerva's magic bridle turned the wild Pegasus into a tame and gentle horse. He sailed gently down to a mountain top. There he stood quietly. Bellerophon slid off his back. Bellerophon threw his arms around the horse's neck.

"Pegasus," he cried, "you are the most beautiful horse in the world! You ought to be free to fly where you wish. I don't want to use the bridle on you, but we must kill the dragon. When we have killed it, I shall set you free."

Bellerophon and Pegasus stayed on the mountain top a few days longer. Bellerophon trained Pegasus to obey him. Pegasus always seemed to know what Bellerophon wanted him to do. After a few days they were ready for the dragon.

Early one morning they set off for Lycia. As they flew over the land they saw burned houses and dead cattle.

"The dragon has been here, Pegasus," cried Bellerophon. "Go slowly now. We must find his hiding place. He must be near."

They sailed slowly over some rough hills. Suddenly Bellerophon saw three clouds of smoke. They came from a big cave in the hills. Pegasus headed downward to the mouth of the cave. The smoke grew thicker. A terrible roar came from the cave. Out of the cloud of smoke flashed the giant head of a lion, from another part, the head of a great snake. Now he saw the horns of a goat. Bellerophon's eyes were burning and he could hardly see. Great clouds of hot smoke poured from the animal's mouths. Bellerophon spoke.

"It's the dragon, Pegasus!" he cried.

Pegasus gave a loud cry and leaped forward. The dragon rushed to meet him. Great flames now burst from all three mouths. Bellerophon had to throw his arm over his eyes. As the dragon made its leap, Pegasus sprang away. In a moment horse and rider were out of reach in the sky.

Bellerophon patted his horse.

"You saved us, Pegasus," he whispered. "But we must go back. We must kill the dragon."

Down, down, they sailed again, straight at the dragon. Just as they were about to crash into him, Pegasus turned aside. They swept by so fast that Bellerophon could hardly see. As they turned he cut hard with his sharp sword. The dragon screamed. In the sky again, Bellerophon looked back. The goat head was rolling down the hill. The lion roared and the snake hissed. The wounded dragon roared in pain.

Again Pegasus flew downward. Again Bellerophon's great sword swung through the smoke and flame. The dragon's sharp claws raked Bellerophon and Pegasus. Again Bellerophon looked back. The lion head was hanging. The flame died out and a last cloud of smoke arose. Both Bellerophon and Pegasus were bleeding. Pegasus turned and went down again. The dragon was rolling over in pain. The big tail swung back and forth. The jaws were open wide.

Bellerophon pulled his sword back. This time he ran it straight into the snake's throat. Pegasus flashed upward again. When Bellerophon looked back the terrible dragon lay still. A cloud of smoke rose slowly.

Bellerophon and Pegasus came back down. They lay down to rest. At last Bellerophon reached over to pat the horse. How he wished he might keep him always! But Bellerophon had made a promise.

"Let's go back to the mountain, Pegasus," he said.

The wonderful horse leaped upward again. In a few minutes they landed.

"Oh, Pegasus, I hate to leave you," cried Bellerophon. "But you have done your work. Now you are free again."

He took the golden bridle from the horse's mouth. With one great leap the horse was gone. Bellerophon watched until he was a black dot in the sky. Then he rubbed his eyes. The black dot was growing larger! In a minute Pegasus was back. He came over to Bellerophon and laid his head on the man's shoulder. Pegasus did not want to leave him!

"Pegasus!" he cried. He threw his arms around the horse's neck and hugged him. Gently the horse licked his face.

Bellerophon was a great hero in Lycia. The king and the people were overjoyed to hear of the dragon's death.

Many years later Jupiter, the king of the gods, wanted to put Pegasus up in the sky. He sent a fly to sting the horse. When the fly stung Pegasus, he jumped. He jumped so suddenly Bellerophon fell off. Pegasus flew up into the sky. There, the Greeks said, he has been ever since.

The SIX POMEGRANATE SEEDS

Today we know why we have changes in the seasons. The earth travels around the sun. It takes the earth a year to travel around the sun once. We have winter when the earth is traveling over one part of its path. We have summer when the earth is traveling over another part of its path.

The Greeks did not know that the earth travels around the sun. They explained the change in seasons with this story. One of the goddesses in the story is named Ceres. From her name we get our word "cereal."

Ceres was the goddess of the harvest. She made the flowers bloom and the crops grow. She was Jupiter's sister. Ceres had a daughter, Proserpine. She loved Proserpine more than anything in the world.

One day Ceres and Proserpine were walking in the fields. Ceres grew tired. She sat down to rest on a hilltop.

"I'll pick some flowers for you while you rest," said Proserpine. She picked some roses near by. Then she saw a daisy field at the foot of the hill. She ran down the hill to pick them. She sang as she went.

Suddenly a wagon pulled by four black horses came down the road. A big man stood in the wagon. Proserpine was too frightened to move. The man stared at the child. Without a word, he reached down and grabbed her. The flowers fell from her hands.

"Mother! Mother!" she cried. "Help, Mother! Help!"

Ceres heard the cries. She ran down the hill. She was too late. She saw only the flowers Proserpine had dropped.

"Someone has run off with my child!" she cried. Her voice shook.

By this time Proserpine and the strange man were far away. Proserpine looked at the man. What she saw frightened her more. He was very big with black hair and dark eyes.

"I want to go home." Her voice shook as she spoke.

"I am Pluto, king of the underworld," the big man said. "I have been watching you. I live where it is lonely and dark. I need a happy little girl like you to live with me. You will brighten my palace."

"But my mother!" the child cried. "She won't know where I am. I must go home."

Just then the horses stopped before some big gates. A dog with three heads stood beside the gates. Proserpine cried out when he growled. His growls were very loud, for they came from all three mouths.

Pluto spoke and the dog was quiet.

"He will not hurt you, child — not unless you try to run away. He is here to watch the gates. Only those who try to get through are hurt."

The gates opened and the horses ran

through. They went deep into the earth. The underworld was far below. It was even farther below than Vulcan's workshop. The horses ran at a terrible speed. They did not stop again until they came to Pluto's palace. Pluto carried Proserpine to the door.

"Welcome to my palace," he said. "Everything will be done to make you happy. You may have anything you want."

"All I want is to go home," said Proserpine. "I can never be happy here. Won't you please take me home?"

"But here you can be a queen," said Pluto. "See all the beautiful things in my palace. They are all yours now."

"I don't want to be a queen," cried Proserpine. "It's too dark down here. Where is the sunshine?"

Pluto did not answer. He placed Proserpine on the throne next to his.

"Bring the little queen the finest food in the palace," he ordered.

Proserpine ate nothing.

"Well, then, bring out the finest clothes,"

he said. "You like pretty clothes, don't you, Proserpine?"

Nothing made her happy.

Back on the earth, Ceres was looking for her little girl. Day after day she looked. She forgot her work as goddess of the harvest. The corn did not ripen. The flowers did not bloom. At last Jupiter sent for Ceres.

"Ceres," he said, "you cannot do this to the earth. It is your work to see that the crops grow."

"Help me find my daughter," said Ceres. "Bring her back to me. Then I will work again."

"I can tell you where Proserpine is," answered Jupiter. "Pluto took her to the underworld. I do not know if I can bring her back to you."

"You are king of the gods. If you know where Proserpine is, why can't you bring her back to me? Pluto has no right to her!"

"I know that, Ceres. But if Proserpine has eaten any food, she cannot come back.

No one who eats below the earth can ever return. I will send Mercury to the underworld. He will find out if Proserpine has eaten anything."

While Jupiter was saying this, Proserpine was on her throne in the underworld. Pluto stood before her. In his hands was a bright red fruit.

"This is a pomegranate," he said. "It is very good. I know you are hungry. Eat it, my child. It will not hurt you."

Proserpine looked at the fruit. She had never seen a pomegranate before. It looked good. And she *was* hungry.

"I'll try one bite," she said. But the pomegranate was full of seeds. Proserpine did not like it.

"I don't want any more," she said. "I swallowed some of the seeds."

Just as she pushed the fruit aside, Mercury came in.

"How did you get here, Mercury?" said Pluto.

"Never mind that! Jupiter sent me. I came to see Proserpine. Tell me, child, have you eaten since you have been here?"

"Just one bite of this pomegranate. That's all."

Mercury said no more. He left as quickly as he had come. He flew back to Jupiter.

After listening to Mercury, Jupiter went to see Pluto. Jupiter felt sorry for Ceres. Besides, he knew there would be no harvest so long as Ceres was unhappy.

He said to Pluto, "I know that anyone who eats while in the underworld cannot return to earth. But Proserpine ate only one bite of a pomegranate. She swallowed six seeds. Will you let her come back to her mother for six months each year? The other six months she will stay with you."

"I want Proserpine forever," answered Pluto. "But I know she is not happy in the underworld. I will let her spend half the year on earth with her mother. Then she will not be so unhappy with me."

So every year Proserpine returns to the earth with the spring. The flowers and the trees grow then. All summer she plays in the fields with her mother. In the autumn she goes back to the underworld. Then Ceres is sad and nothing grows.

The

GORGON'S

HEAD

Perseus was one of the bravest Greek heroes. When he was just a little boy, his father died. His father was a king. So it was right that Perseus should be the next king. There were some bad men who did not want this. They said, "Let us build a big box. We will take Perseus and his mother far out to sea in it. They will drown. Then we can choose our own king."

Perseus and his mother saw the men.

"What do you want?" cried the frightened mother. "Where are you taking us?"

The men did not answer.

"Why are you putting us in this box?" the mother asked.

Still the men did not answer. They tied the box to their boat. They rowed far out to sea. Then they cut loose the box.

"Please do not leave us!" cried the mother. "We will drown. What have we done? Why do you want us to die?"

The men were already out of sight. The wind blew hard. The waves tossed the box up and down. Perseus and his mother did not drown. The box floated to an island. There a fisherman caught it in his net. The fisherman took Perseus and his mother to his house. He gave them food and dry clothes.

"You are very kind," said Perseus' mother. "Let me tell you our story. Cruel men left us to drown. We cannot go home. Will you let us stay here?"

The fisherman was glad to let them stay. For many years they lived happily together.

One day when Perseus' mother was in the garden the king rode by. He stopped to talk with her. After that, he stopped to see her many times. Once he ordered her to come to the palace. There he said to her,

"I have been watching you for a long time. Will you marry me and be my queen?"

Perseus' mother was too surprised to answer right away. At last she said, "I cannot marry you. My son needs me. I must stay with him."

Now this king was not good and kind. He was really a very evil man. The woman's answer made him angry. Few people said no to him. For days he thought of ways to get rid of Perseus. He felt sure she would marry him if the boy were gone. At last he thought of a wicked plan. He sent for Perseus.

"Perseus," he said. "You grew up in my country. My people have been kind to you. Would you like to do something for us?"

Perseus said just what the king wanted him to say.

"Oh, yes. I will do anything you ask! How can I repay you?"

The wicked king was ready with his answer.

"I am glad you are such a fine, brave

boy. This will be a great adventure for you. There are three fierce animals called Gorgons living not far from here. One of them is killing our people. If she were dead, I should be very happy."

Perseus did not stop to think. He wanted to do something for the king. He wanted to show he was brave.

"I can do it!" he cried. "I'll kill the Gorgon! I'll bring back her head! If I don't, you will never see me again."

After the boy left, the king laughed. His plan had worked. He was sure Perseus would never come back.

These Gorgons were terrible beasts. They had big, sharp teeth and brass claws. Live snakes grew on their heads. Their skin was so tough nothing could go through it. They had wings, too. The worst thing about them was this: anyone who looked at a Gorgon's face turned to stone. No wonder the king thought he would never see Perseus again!

Early the next morning Perseus started on his dangerous adventure. While he was walking, he began to think. Suddenly it came to him. The king had tricked him!

"How foolish I am," he said. "I can't kill a Gorgon. The Gorgons will kill me. Why did I make such a promise?"

Then he heard a voice behind him saying, "Perseus, why are you worried?"

He turned around. There stood a man wearing a cape and a strange cap. Perseus looked at him closely. He saw tiny wings on his cap. They were on his feet, too. Perseus knew he was Mercury, the gods' messenger.

"Tell me why you are worried, Perseus," Mercury said again. "Maybe I can help you."

Mercury listened while Perseus told his story.

"Yes," he said when Perseus had finished. "You were foolish. But I will help you. If you listen to me, you can get the Gorgon's head. First of all, you must shine your shield. Shine it until you can see your face in it."

Perseus did as he was told. "That's fine,"

Mercury said. "Now take my sword. It is the only sword that can cut off the Gorgon's head. Our first job is to find the three gray sisters."

"The three gray sisters!" cried Perseus. So far Mercury's advice seemed silly. "Who are the three sisters? I've never heard of them."

"They are three very strange old women," said Mercury. "They have only one eye among them. They pass the eye back and forth. First one sister slips the eye into her head and looks around. Then she hands it to the next sister. They fight a lot about whose turn it is to have the eye."

By this time it was growing dark. Mercury and Perseus had been walking as they talked.

"Here we are," whispered Mercury. "This is the cave where the sisters live."

"What must I do," asked Perseus, "now that we've found them?"

"You must watch your chance to get the eye. When one sister passes the eye to the other, step in between them and take it.

Sh—— listen! You can hear them talking. They are coming this way."

"Sister! Sister!" one of them was saying. "You have had the eye long enough."

"Let me keep it just another minute."

"No! Give it to me! It's my turn now!"

Here the third sister spoke up. "I should have the eye next! You two always want to keep it to yourselves and it's not fair!"

With that, the sister who had the eye jerked it out and held it in her hand.

"Here, take it, one of you," she cried, "and stop your quarreling."

At that instant, Perseus leaped from behind the tree where he and Mercury had been hiding. He grabbed the eye.

"Who stole our eye? Give us back our eye!" they cried. "It is our only eye! We cannot see."

"Tell them," whispered Mercury to Perseus, "that they shall have their eye when they tell you where to find the Nymphs."

"I will give you back your eye," said Perseus to the three gray sisters, "if you tell me something. Where are the Nymphs?"

The sisters wanted their eye badly enough to tell Perseus anything. Quickly they told him what he wanted to know. He gave back their eye.

"Tell me who the Nymphs are," said Perseus to Mercury after they left the gray sisters.

"The Nymphs are young women. They have three gifts for you. Without their gifts, you cannot hope to kill the Gorgon."

It did not take Mercury and Perseus long to find the Nymphs. They gave Perseus the three gifts. One gift was a magic leather purse. Another was a pair of shoes with wings on them. The last gift was a strange cap. When Perseus wore the cap, no one could see him. Wearing the shoes, he could fly.

"You will need the purse, too," said Mercury. "Now that you have these gifts you are ready to fight the Gorgon."

They went straight to the Gorgons' cave. There were the Gorgons, fast asleep.

"Now is your time," said Mercury. "Be quick. If they wake up, it will be too late.

Only one can be killed. That is Medusa. She's the middle one. Be sure not to look at her. Use your shield as a mirror. That's why I told you to shine it. Hurry!"

Perseus flew down. He struck hard at Medusa with his sword. Off came the terrible head!

"Put it in your purse," called Mercury.

To Perseus' surprise, the small purse grew large enough to hold Medusa's head. The other Gorgons awoke. They tried to scratch Perseus with their claws. Quickly he put on his magic cap. No longer could the Gorgons see him.

Perseus looked around. Mercury was gone. He hurried to the king.

"You!" cried the king when he saw Perseus. "What are you doing here?"

"I have come back from the Gorgons' cave. I killed Medusa."

"How do I know you are telling the truth?" asked the king. "You said you would bring back the head. Show it to me."

"All right!" said Perseus. He held the

head before the king's eyes. The king turned to stone. Perseus put the head back in his purse. Then he went to find his mother. The wicked king would bother her no more.

The
HUNDRED-EYED
ARGUS

Everyone knew that Juno, the queen of the gods, was jealous. Jupiter was the only one who was not afraid of her. He often liked other women. This always made Juno angry. She could not punish Jupiter. She always punished the one he thought beautiful. This happened to a young girl named Io.

Jupiter said he thought Io was beautiful. Someone told Juno.

"He thinks she is beautiful, does he?" she said. "I'll fix that! Wait until I find her!"

Now Jupiter had to think fast. He did not want Juno to punish Io. So he changed the young woman into a beautiful white cow.

"Juno will never find her now," he said. "She will forget about it. Then I'll change Io back into a young woman."

But Juno was very wise. She saw the beautiful white cow. She knew it was Io.

"I see a white cow on the earth," she said to Jupiter. "I have never seen one so beautiful. I want it for a pet."

Poor Jupiter had to give Juno the cow. He could think of no good reason for saying no.

Then Juno sent for Argus. Argus was a strange, ugly man. Instead of two eyes, he had a hundred eyes. They were all over his body — even on his arms and legs. Some of his eyes were blue. Some were brown. Some were green. Every one of them had an evil look.

"Argus, I want you to watch that white cow," said Juno. "She is my pet. You are never to leave her. Follow her wherever she goes. Don't let her out of your sight."

That was an easy job for Argus. Only

two of his eyes closed at a time. The other ninety-eight stayed open.

Io went from place to place. Argus was always near by. His terrible eyes watched her day and night.

High on Olympus, Jupiter thought about Io. He felt sorry for her.

"After all, it is my fault," he said. "Juno punished her because I said she was beautiful. I must help her. But how?"

He sent for Mercury, the messenger of the gods.

"See that white cow?" he said to Mercury. "She is really the beautiful girl, Io. That terrible Argus follows her everywhere. I want you to kill him. Do you think you can?"

"I will try," said the brave Mercury. "I'll have to take him by surprise. It won't be easy to surprise a man with a hundred eyes."

Mercury dressed as a shepherd. In his belt he put a short sword. He carried a music pipe. All shepherds played on these pipes. They played to quiet the sheep.

When he was dressed, he flew down to the earth. Seeing Argus and Io, he walked toward them. He played a little tune as he walked. It was sweet, soft music. Even the Hundred-Eyed Argus listened. He did not know this shepherd was really a god.

"I like your music," he said.

"Thank you, sir," said Mercury. "Would you like to hear some more?"

"Play all the songs you know. I like to listen to music. Come, sit beside me."

At first Mercury's music was fast. Then he changed to soft, sleepy tunes. One eye of Argus closed, then another. Mercury played on. At last only one eye was open. Now Mercury's music was very soft. He played the sweetest tune he knew. Just as the music ended, the eye closed. All hundred eyes were shut. Argus was asleep!

Quick as lightning, Mercury jumped up. He took the sword from his belt. With one blow, he cut off Argus' head. Io was free from the hundred watching eyes.

"How can I thank you?" Io cried. "You are not a shepherd. Tell me your name."

"I am Mercury. Jupiter sent me to kill Argus. I wish I could change you into a woman again. If I did, Juno would really be angry. But at least Argus will no longer watch you."

Juno was angry enough when she heard that Argus was dead.

"Go to the body," she ordered. "Take the hundred eyes from it. Bring them here to me. I will put them in my peacock's tail. They will always be there to remind Jupiter of Argus. He will not be so quick to call other women beautiful."

The Greeks said the beautiful spots in a peacock's tail were really the eyes of Argus.

The
BIG and
LITTLE BEAR

Do you know the Big Dipper when you see it in the sky? The star map beside the story shows you how it looks. There are seven bright stars in it. These seven stars are part of a larger group of stars called "The Great Bear." The handle of the Dipper is the Great Bear's tail. The cup of the Dipper is a part of the Bear's body. Look for the two large stars on the outside edge of the Dipper. They are called "The Pointers." They point to the North Star.

The North Star is in the group of stars called the Little Dipper. The Little Dipper has another name, too. Sometimes it is called "The Little Bear." Look again at the star map. The North Star is the last star in the handle of the Little Dipper. The handle of the Little Dipper is the tail of the Little Bear. It is easier to find the North Star in the sky if you let the "Pointers" help you.

The North Star is a very important star. People tell directions from it. Most of the stars rise and set just as the sun and moon do. But the North Star does not rise or set. If you were at the North Pole, the North Star would be right over your head. The North Star is right above the North Pole. Because of this, it stays in the same place in the sky. The earth spins around, but the North Star does not move.

The stars near the North Star do not rise or set either. The turning of the earth seems to make them move in the sky. But they never leave the sky.

The Greeks explained the rising and setting of the stars another way. They thought when the stars rose, they were coming out of the sea. When they set, they were going into the sea.

The Greeks told a story about the Great Bear and the Little Bear. They said that the Great Bear was once a beautiful girl. Her name was Callisto. The Little Bear was once a boy named Arcas. Arcas was Callisto's young son.

One day Jupiter looked down at the earth. He saw Callisto.

"How beautiful she is! I could watch her all day," he said.

Jupiter never tired of looking at beautiful women. This always made his wife, Juno, angry. She did not want him to like other women.

"What is so beautiful about Callisto?" asked Juno. "She is just an earth woman. I don't think she is so pretty. All the goddesses are more beautiful than she."

The great Jupiter did not listen. Thoughtfully he smoothed his beard.

"She is almost as beautiful as a goddess," he said.

This made Juno really angry. Jupiter was not even listening to her. "I'll keep him from seeing her again," Juno said to herself. "Callisto likes to hunt. I'll wait until she is in the forest alone. Then I'll change her into a big black bear."

One day when Callisto was hunting alone, she began to feel strange. And no wonder! She looked at her hands. They were broad hairy feet. She saw that she was covered with thick black hair. Trying to call for help, she found her voice was a roar. The beautiful woman had become a great black bear.

Juno was watching. She sat on Mt. Olympus laughing. "Jupiter will not call her beautiful now," she said.

Poor Callisto! She was afraid of the other animals. And she had to hide from the hunters. She went about the forest alone. One day she saw a young hunter walking toward her. It was her own son — Arcas! She tried to call out to him. But she could only growl. She ran to him. She was so happy to see him. She forgot that Arcas would not know her.

"Oh, my son!" she growled. "How good it is to see you again!"

Of course, Arcas was very much afraid. He did not know this was his mother. All he could see was a large black bear growling at him. Raising his spear he started to fight it.

Just at this moment Jupiter looked down. He saw what was happening.

"Something must be done," he cried. "Arcas cannot kill his own mother!"

As quickly as Juno changed Callisto, Jupiter changed Arcas. He became a smaller bear. Jupiter then put the two bears among the stars in the sky.

"They will be safe there," he said.

When Juno saw what Jupiter had done, she was very angry. She sent for Neptune, the god of the sea.

"See what Jupiter has done," said the queen of the gods. "I changed Callisto from a woman to a bear. Jupiter changed her son into a bear, too. Now he has put them both among the stars. They should not get such an honor. You must do something to help me."

"I cannot change Jupiter's work," the

god answered. "But I will do this. They shall never rest beneath the water with the other stars."

Ever since that time, the Great Bear and the Little Bear have never rested. They wander about in a circle in the sky.

ATALANTA

Atalanta was the daughter of a king. When she was born, her father did not want her. He wanted a son — not a daughter. He took her to a lonely forest. There he left her to die.

Some hunters heard the baby crying. They took her to their home. For many years she lived with them. They loved the little girl. They taught her to hunt with a bow and arrows. Soon she could shoot as well as any hunter. They taught her how to run. She learned to run faster than anything in the forest. Even the wild animals could not outrun Atalanta. The hunters talked about her to everyone.

"Have you ever seen our beautiful girl?" they would say. "She runs as fast as the wind." Many young people in the town ran races with Atalanta. No one ever beat her.

At last the king himself heard about her. "Bring her to me," he said. "I want to see this girl who can run so fast. She must race for me."

When Atalanta stood before the king, she said, "What do you want of me, sir?"

"First I want to know who you are."

"I do not know, sir," answered Atalanta. "When I was a baby, I was left in the forest. Some kind hunters found me. They took care of me. I have lived with them ever since. I do not know about my father and mother. I do not even know my name."

The king asked her more questions. When he heard her answers, he knew she was his daughter.

"You are my daughter — Atalanta!" he cried. "Forgive me for what I did. I was wrong to want a son so much. Now I want my daughter. I'm an old man. The palace is lonely. Please say you will come live with me. I will try to make you happy. Your friends who took care of you may live here, too."

"I forgive you," said Atalanta. "I would like to live with you."

Atalanta was a very beautiful young girl. Before long, many young men wanted to marry her. Atalanta liked her new life in the palace. She was in no hurry to marry. So she said, "I will marry the man who can run faster than I. Anyone wishing to marry me must race with me. If he wins, I will marry him. If he loses, he must die!"

Many of the young men had heard about Atalanta. They knew how fast she could run. Not wishing to die, they gave up and went home. Others tried and lost. They paid with their lives.

One day a tall, handsome young man came to see the king. While he was in the palace, he met Atalanta. He fell in love with her. He asked her to marry him.

"Anyone who wants to marry me must

first beat me in a race," said Atalanta. "If he loses, he is put to death. Surely you do not want to die. Why risk your life for me?"

"You are very beautiful, Atalanta. If I can win the race, you will be my wife. I'd like to try."

The race was set for the next day. That night the young man called to the goddess, Venus.

"You are the goddess of love and beauty," he said. "Will you help me win the lovely Atalanta?"

Venus heard him. She went to her garden and picked three beautiful golden apples. These she brought to the young man.

"Take these apples," she said. "I will whisper what you are to do with them. Listen well."

Early the next morning Atalanta and the young man lined up for the race. A crowd gathered to watch. They all hoped the boy would win. Even Atalanta wished he might run faster than she.

The arrow was shot into the air. This

was the sign for the race to begin. Atalanta was soon far ahead. The people shouted to the young man, "Faster! Run faster! You can do it!"

The boy was doing his best. But Atalanta was far in front. At that moment he threw one of the golden apples. He threw it so that it rolled to the feet of Atalanta.

To everyone's surprise she stopped to pick it up. The boy took the lead.

Shouts came again from the crowd, "You're ahead! You're ahead! Keep going and you can win!"

He was not ahead for long. Again Atalanta passed him. Again he threw an apple. Atalanta slowed down. Quietly the crowd watched. Then again she stopped to pick up the apple. The boy passed her.

By this time the crowd was shouting wildly. Never before had they seen such a race!

The young man was getting tired. He began to fall behind. He had but one apple left. He hoped Venus would guide him when he threw it. It landed just ahead of

Atalanta. Then it rolled a little to one side. To get it, Atalanta had to stop and turn aside. It gave the boy just time enough to pass her and win the race. The crowd shouted until they could shout no more.

Atalanta kept her promise to marry the winner of the race. To tell the truth, she was glad he won.

The

GOLDEN
FLEECE

There was great trouble in a little country near Greece. The king of the country was a kind man who ruled well. But his wicked brother wanted to be king. When he saw his chance, he made himself king. He was cruel and selfish, but the people could not help themselves.

The real king had a son named Jason. When Jason grew up, he would become king. The bad uncle did not want Jason.

"My own son shall be king," he said. "I will make sure he does. Jason must die."

Jason's father found out what the evil brother wanted to do. "I will save the boy," he said. "I will send him far away.

The centaurs are my friends. I will send Jason to the land of the centaurs." Now the centaurs were strange people. They had the bodies of horses, but from the waist up they were men. They could run like the wind and were great fighters.

The most famous centaur was Chiron. Chiron was a famous teacher. Many kings' sons came to him to learn. He taught them to ride and shoot and fight. Chiron was glad to see Jason. "A son of my old friend!" he cried. "I shall teach you all I know." The wise Chiron did teach Jason for years. At last Chiron said, "My boy, you have learned well. I can teach you no more. Your father needs you. Go home. You must become king instead of your wicked uncle."

"Are you sure I am ready to be king?" asked Jason. "I know my people need me. How shall I overcome my uncle?"

"You are ready, Jason," said Chiron. "I think the gods will show you the way. Do not be afraid."

Jason started the next morning. He wore

a lion's skin over his shoulder. In each hand he carried a spear. On his feet were a pair of low shoes called sandals. Jason was proud of those sandals. His father had given them to him.

Jason was a fine-looking young man. But even for those times, he looked strange. Young men did not wear lions' skins. So people stared at him as he passed.

"Look," they said, "a fellow wearing a lion's skin. Who can he be? Where can he be going?"

Jason did not answer. He kept walking. He traveled many miles. One day he came to a swift stream. "How can I get across?" he thought. "It's too deep to wade. It's too wide to swim."

He stood on the bank thinking. Suddenly he heard a voice behind him. "Jason!" said the voice. He turned quickly. An ugly old woman stood behind him. She wore old ragged clothes. She leaned on a queer looking stick. "Young man," she said. "I must cross this stream. I cannot do it alone. You look strong. Will you carry me across?"

He thought, "I don't know how I'm going to get across myself. How does the silly old woman think I can get her over?" He was about to tell her no. Then he remembered Chiron. He could almost hear Chiron saying, "You must always be kind to the old and the poor."

"I'll try," he said quickly. "I'm not sure I can make it. But I'll try. Get on my back. We'll see how strong I really am."

He helped the old lady get on his back. He stepped into the stream. The water rushed swiftly around his feet. He took a last look over his shoulder. What he saw surprised him. Seated on the old woman's shoulder was a peacock! Jason started to say something. Then he stopped.

"The middle of a stream is no place to talk," he said to himself. "I must get her across safely."

Every step was dangerous. He used his two spears to keep from falling. Once he caught his foot in some rocks. Pulling it loose, he lost his sandal. Before he could stop, the water carried it away.

"There goes my sandal," he cried. "It was all I had from my father."

"Do not worry, Jason," the old lady said, smiling. Even as she was speaking, she began to change. Soon she was no longer an ugly old woman. She changed into a beautiful young girl. Jason stared at her.

"Do not worry about your sandal," she went on. "Losing it was good luck. You have lost your sandal, but you have found a friend. The goddess Juno never forgets a kindness."

Followed by her peacock, she went out of sight. Jason looked after her. "Juno!" he cried. "Juno, queen of the gods! That's how I got across the stream. Juno helped me. But how about the sandal? How could losing it be good luck? Well, Juno is a goddess. She ought to know. I guess I'll find out when I get to the king."

He walked more slowly now. The bare foot made walking harder. At last he came to his own country. The houses looked so different. Everything seemed strange. He was sure no one knew him. Yet everyone stared as he passed.

Stopping a man, he asked, "Where is the palace? I must find the king."

The man started to answer. Then he looked more closely at Jason.

"Look at him!" he shouted. "Look at him. He wears only one sandal!"

Jason tried to hide his bare foot. He did not know what to do. More people gathered around him. They all shouted.

"He wears one sandal! Here's the man with one sandal. He's come at last."

"What of it?" cried Jason angrily. "Can't a man wear one sandal if he wants to?" Then he remembered that Juno had said, "Do not worry about your sandal. Losing it was good luck."

"Let them look," he said. "I'll soon find out what's the matter." He started walking again toward the palace. Great crowds of people followed him. When they came to the palace, the king saw the crowd and came out. When they saw the king, the crowd began to back away. Jason stood alone.

"Now it has happened," the king said to himself. "The man with one sandal has come."

Both the king and the crowd knew the story of the man with one shoe. Long ago a wise man had told the king he would lose his crown.

"A man wearing one shoe will take it," the wise man had said. "He will become king in your place."

Now he was here — the man with one shoe. The people knew it. The king knew it. What was the evil king to do?

"I must get rid of him," he said to himself. To Jason he said, "Who are you, young man? What do you want?"

"My name is Jason," answered the boy. "I am the son of the real king of the country. I have come to claim the throne. It belongs to me."

The crowd grew quiet. Everyone listened for the king's answer.

"Of course, Jason," he said. "I am glad

to see you. I have been waiting. I have kept the kingdom for you. As soon as you are ready, you shall be king."

"I have lived with Chiron," Jason said. "He has taught me many things. I think I am ready to be king. I will be kind to my people. I will try to rule wisely."

But the wicked king was not ready to give up. Already he was planning to get rid of Jason.

He said, "Did Chiron teach you everything? Let me see how clever you are. Did he tell you what to do if someone wanted your throne? What would you do?"

Before he thought, Jason answered. "I'd send him to get the Golden Fleece," he said with a laugh.

As soon as the words were spoken the king smiled. Jason saw how the king had tricked him. But it was too late.

"You are very wise, my boy," said the king. "That is a good test. Chiron taught you well. When you bring me the Golden Fleece, you may be king."

Now the Golden Fleece was the skin of

a wonderful sheep. This sheep had saved two children. In honor of its good deed, it was turned to gold. Sparkling and shining, the gold skin was hung on a tree in a far away land. Everyone wanted it. Heroes tried to get it for their kings. Many lost their lives trying. Now it was Jason's turn.

To get the Golden Fleece, Jason would have to make a long trip over dangerous seas. He would need a good strong ship. He went to Argus, the ship builder, an old friend of his father. Argus built the world's best ships. He was glad to see Jason again.

"Argus," said Jason, "I need your help. I am going on a long trip. I am going to bring home the Golden Fleece. I need a big strong ship. Will you build it for me?"

"I will build it, Jason. I will build you the largest ship ever built. You will need fifty strong men to row it. By the time you get your men, I will have your ship ready."

Jason began making plans. He sent messengers all over the kingdom. "Go talk to the young men," he told them. "Tell them Jason, their real king, needs them. Take only the forty-nine strongest and bravest."

Many young men wanted to go with Jason. They hated his uncle, the wicked king. They wanted Jason to rule. Besides, they liked the idea of adventure. They saw a chance to prove their bravery.

When they were chosen, Jason was very proud. He had a fine crew. They were the strongest and bravest young men in the country. They called themselves the Argonauts. Their ship was named the Argos, for its builder, Argus.

The Argonauts set sail on their journey. Their adventures started soon after they sailed. The ship almost crashed on some rocks. Next they met some cruel giants. The giants tried to eat them alive. Later terrible birds flew over them. The birds shot their sharp pointed feathers at them. But a greater danger was coming.

By now they had come near the country of the Golden Fleece. Before they could land, two men rowed out to their ship. The men in the small boat begged the Argonauts to go home.

"Go back," they said. "Go back before it is too late. There is much danger ahead. The Golden Fleece is guarded well. A great dragon watches it. He kills everyone who comes near him. It would be terrible for all of you to be killed. Go home while you have a chance."

"If any of my men wishes to turn back, he may go," Jason said. "I must go on. I cannot go back home without the Golden Fleece."

The Argonauts spoke up. "Not one of us will turn back," they cried. "We are not afraid of a dragon or any other danger. We'll stay, Jason, every one of us."

So they went ashore. Straight to the king they went. He was surprised to see them. But he said, "Welcome, brave Jason. What brings you to our land?"

"I have come for the Golden Fleece," Jason said. "I must have it to get my kingdom from my uncle."

Now the king was proud of the Golden Fleece. He did not want to give it up. So he frowned at Jason. "Anyone searching for the Golden Fleece must pass some hard tests. He must first tame two fierce bulls. These bulls breathe out fire. Their breath is so hot no one dares get close to them. Everyone who has tried has been burned to death. Their horns are very sharp too. Do you still want to go on?"

"I must go on. If the bulls must be tamed, I will tame them," said Jason.

"Taming them isn't all," the king went on. "After they are tamed, you must plow with them. You must plant some dragon teeth. From each tooth you plant will come a soldier. You and your men must fight them. You will all be killed."

Jason was not frightened. He would not give up. "No we won't," said Jason. "We are not afraid to fight."

While the king was talking, a young girl came up beside him. When Jason left she followed him.

"I am the king's daughter Medea," she said. "I can help you. If you do what I say, you can get the Golden Fleece."

Jason needed all the help he could get.

So he said, "I'll be glad to do anything you say. We need help."

Medea gave him two boxes. "Remember the old woman you carried on your back? She gave me these boxes for you. One holds oil. It will keep you from being burned by the bulls' flaming breath. The second you will use on the dragon. The third thing I will whisper in your ear."

She whispered to Jason. Then she led him to the big black bulls. The fire curled from their noses. It burned everything near them. Jason stopped to rub the oil on his skin. Then he stepped into the field. The bulls saw him at once. Tails standing straight out, they rushed at him. Flames danced around them as they ran. Jason waited calmly for them to come close.

The flames soon were all around him. But the magic oil saved him. He was not burned. Now the bulls lowered their heads. They charged him with their sharp horns. Just as they reached him, he moved quickly. Reaching out, he grabbed a horn of each bull. The great bulls tossed their heads, but Jason hung on. He felt new strength in his arms. "It must be Juno again," he thought. Slowly he twisted the bulls' heads. At last he held them helpless. They became quiet and gentle. Jason let them loose. He tied them to the plow which stood in the field.

Taking the dragon's teeth from Medea, he began to plant them. As soon as a tooth fell, a fierce soldier sprang up. They rushed at Jason. But he remembered the words Medea had whispered to him. Stooping over, he picked up a stone. He threw it into the middle of the soldiers. It flew from the helmet of one to the shield of another. Each thought the other had struck him.

"Why do you hit me?" cried one.

"You hit me!" said another.

Soon they were all fighting. They fought among themselves until everyone was dead. Jason stood aside until the battle ended.

Now two of the big dangers were past. Jason was getting closer to the Golden Fleece. He could see it, far away, shining in the sun. In his hurry to get closer, he forgot the dragon. But not for long. Suddenly, before him rose a terrible neck and head. It waved back and forth in the air, spitting fire.

Jason held tight to the box Medea had given him. Closer and closer to the dragon he crept.

"I'll wait for the right moment," he said. "Then I'll use the box. It is my only chance."

Just then the moment came. The ugly head struck at him. The mouth opened to grab him in the terrible jaws. But into the mouth went the little box. Jason threw it with all his strength. The dragon fell back. Out of its mouth came one awful cry. Then it curled up and died.

Jason lost no time. He quickly grabbed the Golden Fleece. Hurrying back to his ship, he stopped to thank Medea.

"Take me with you!" she cried.

"Come," said Jason.

He took her hand. Together they hurried to the ship.

His men saw them coming. They shouted

with joy. "Our search is over. We have found the Golden Fleece. Now we can go home. Jason shall be king!"

As soon as Jason and Medea were on board, the ship sailed. After more adventures, they reached home safely. Jason went to the king.

"Uncle, I have found the Golden Fleece. It is yours when you give me my kingdom."

The king wanted the Golden Fleece. He did not want to give up his kingdom. But he had given his promise. All the people had heard him. So Jason became the king and ruled wisely with Medea for many years.

PHAETON

There are many deserts in the world. They are hot dry places. They have no trees or rivers. The Greeks told a story about these deserts. They thought that Phaeton made them. This is the story they told.

Apollo, the sun god, was Phaeton's father. His mother was an earth woman. Apollo lived with the gods on Mt. Olympus. Phaeton and his mother lived on the earth.

Phaeton's mother told him of his father. Each day she pointed to the sun and said, "There goes your father. He is driving the sun across the sky. He is the only one strong enough to drive those horses."

Phaeton was proud of his father. He talked about him all the time. His friends tired of his bragging. One day the boys said, "You're always talking about your father. You say he is Apollo the sun god. You've never even seen him. What proof do you have that he is your father?"

"Apollo is my father! I can prove it all right! I'll go see him. Then you'll believe me!"

The boys laughed and walked away.

Phaeton shouted after them, "You'll be sorry. I'll go see my father. I'll drive his sun horses, too. Then you'll have to believe me. You watch and see!"

The boys heard him. "You have a fine chance of doing that. We'll believe it when we see it."

Phaeton was angry. He rushed home. "Mother, I've got to go see my father. The boys won't believe what I tell them. They laugh when I say Apollo is my father. I've got to prove it to them. I must go see him!"

"It's a long trip, Phaeton. You are

young to make such a trip alone. I am an earth woman. I cannot go with you."

"I am not afraid, mother. I don't want to leave you. But I must go. I've got to prove to those boys that Apollo is my father. Please tell me how to find him."

"You know the earth is shaped like a saucer. The edges are turned up to keep the oceans out. It is to the eastern edge you must go. That is where your father starts his journey with the sun each morning. If you will be very careful, I'll let you go."

Phaeton left at once. He walked as his mother had told him. At last he came to the earth's steep edge. He climbed to the top. There was the palace of the sun god. He knocked on the door. When it opened, he stepped inside. He was in the brightest, most beautiful room he had ever seen. At one end was a throne. On it sat a tall man dressed in purple robes. He spoke to Phaeton.

"Who are you? What do you want in the palace of the sun?"

"I am Phaeton, the son of Apollo. I am looking for my father."

"Welcome, my son. I am Apollo." Apollo left his throne. He came to the boy and greeted him. "You are most welcome, Phaeton. I am glad to see you. But why have you made this long trip?"

"I had to see you, father. My friends do not believe I am your son. I can prove it to them if you will let me do one thing."

"Why, of course, my son. Now that you are here, I'll let you do anything. What is it you want to do?"

Phaeton took a deep breath. His voice shook as he spoke. "I want to drive the sun across the sky."

Apollo stepped back. His face grew dark. "No one, not even Jupiter, can drive those horses. That is the one thing you cannot do. Ask me anything else. But you can't drive the horses of the sun."

"But, father, I told the boys I would. That's the last thing I said to them. You don't love me! If you did, you would let me drive your horses."

Apollo was getting angry. "You are my son," he said. "I love you very much. But you are a foolish boy. No boy can drive those horses."

But Phaeton kept right on. "Do you want people to laugh at your son? Father, you said you would let me do anything."

There was nothing left for Apollo to say or do. Phaeton would not listen. "All right, Phaeton," he said. "You may try. But you will be sorry. Come, I will take you to the horses."

Phaeton could think only of his friends on earth. He could see their faces when they heard about this. They would never laugh at him again! He would show them!

He followed his father from the room. Apollo walked very fast. Phaeton had trouble keeping up with him. In no time they came to the gate.

There were the horses. Phaeton had never seen such horses. They were big and black and wild. Apollo could hardly harness them.

"Are you sure that you still want to go,

Phaeton?" said Apollo. "It is not too late to change your mind."

"Oh, no!" cried Phaeton. "I do not want to change my mind. I've got to drive those horses!"

"Then listen to me, Phaeton. Never use the whip. Hold tight to the reins. Follow my wheel tracks. You must not go too high. If you do, you will burn the homes of the gods. Do not go too low or you will burn the earth. Now, take the reins."

He put the reins in Phaeton's hands. The horses leaped forward. Apollo turned sadly away.

At first Phaeton was excited. The wind rushed past him. The colors rose in the sky. He felt very big and strong.

Then the horses found that the hands on the reins were light and weak. They ran faster and faster. Phaeton braced his feet and tried to pull back. It was no use. He was frightened now. Little by little the reins slipped from his hands. At last he lost them.

Then the horses leaped and galloped.

First they went up past the palaces of the gods. Phaeton grabbed the sides of the cart. It was all he could do to hold on. Then the horses rushed downward. They touched the earth. Cities burst into flame. Fields were burned black. The people ran from their homes. They cried to the gods for help.

On Olympus Jupiter heard their cries. He looked down. Everywhere he saw fire and frightened people. Across the sky the sun horses were still racing. Behind them he saw Phaeton. Something had to be done! The whole world was in danger!

"I must stop this," said Jupiter. "I can think of only one way to do it. So long as Phaeton is in the cart, the horses will not stop. I will have to throw a bolt of lightning at Phaeton."

Jupiter threw the lightning. The bolt hit Phaeton. It knocked him from the cart. Down he fell like a shooting star. Straight into the waters of a deep river he fell. Phaeton was dead. But the world was saved.

The

GOLDEN

TOUCH

Did you ever wish you could have everything you asked for? The Greeks told a story about a king named Midas who did get everything he wanted. Sometimes today we say someone has the "Midas touch." We mean that everything this person does makes money. Sometimes too, we call a very greedy man a "Midas." After reading this story, you will understand why.

The Greeks said that King Midas loved gold more than anything. He did not like to touch or look at anything not made of gold. He loved his crown, but only because it was made of gold. The only other thing he really loved was his daughter Mary.

Midas spent some time with his daughter and some time ruling his people. But most of his time he spent with his gold. He kept it in a secret room under his palace. After locking the door, he loved to sit and look at it. He liked to pile the gold high around him. Over and over he counted his money. Often he looked at his face in a big gold cup. Then he would say, "Oh, Midas, what a happy man you are! You have so much gold!"

One day King Midas was locked in the secret room as usual. Suddenly a shadow fell across the gold. Frightened, he looked up. There stood a strange young man. Midas looked at the door. It was still locked. Now he was really afraid. He looked again at the stranger.

"Are you a god?" he said. "You must be. No one else could get into this locked room."

"Never mind who I am, Midas," said the stranger. "Let's talk about you. You must be a very rich man. I've never seen a room like this before. There must be more gold here than in any other place in the world."

Midas was pleased. But he was still a little frightened.

"Yes," he said, "I've done well. It took me all my life to get this much gold. But to be really rich, I'd have to live a thousand years."

"You mean you aren't satisfied?" asked the visitor. "With all this gold, you should be. What more could you want? I would like to know."

Midas stopped to think. He knew this man must be a god. Gods could do anything. Maybe he would be given a wish. He had a good idea. Raising his head, he looked at the stranger.

"Well, Midas," the stranger said, "I see you have thought of something. Tell me your wish."

"I would be happier," said Midas, "if I had more gold. I am tired of gathering it with so much trouble. I wish everything I touch would turn to gold."

The stranger smiled. "You want everything you touch to turn to gold! That's a strange wish. Are you sure that is what you want? You won't be sorry?"

"Oh, no," answered Midas. "I could never be sorry — not if I had all that gold."

"Then you shall have your wish. Tomorrow at sunrise, you will have the Golden Touch."

A strong light shone around the stranger. Midas had to close his eyes. When he opened them, he was alone again.

That night Midas could not sleep. He was waiting for the sun to rise.

"Perhaps it was all a dream. Maybe I just thought there was someone here. I wish the sun would come up so I would know."

As soon as it began to grow light, Midas started touching things. He touched his pillow. Nothing happened. He touched the covers on his bed. They did not change. "How foolish I am!" he said. "Of course it was just a dream."

Then, as he lay there, a sunbeam shone on the ceiling. The light on the bed covers looked strange. He looked more closely. Under his hand, the covers had turned to gold. Midas jumped up. He ran around the room touching everything. He touched a chair. It turned to gold. He pulled back a curtain. It became heavy in his hand — gold! He picked up a book. At his touch, it became bright gold.

Quickly he dressed. He was pleased to see his suit of fine gold cloth. He took out his handkerchief. Mary had made it for him. That also became gold. For some reason, this did not quite please Midas. He wished that Mary's present had stayed the same. But this did not trouble him very long.

King Midas was happy as he went downstairs. He hurried to the garden. Laughing happily, he changed every flower to gold.

Then he went to breakfast. Mary was waiting. She smiled as he sat down. "Good morning, father. You look very happy this morning."

"I am happy, Mary," he answered. "A

wonderful thing has happened. You will be happy, too, when I tell you. But first let's eat our breakfast."

He poured himself a cup of coffee. He was pleased to see the coffee pot turn to gold. But the surprise came when his lips touched the coffee. First it became yellow. The next minute it was hard gold.

"What's the matter, father?" asked Mary.

"Nothing, dear, nothing!" said Midas. "Eat your breakfast while it's hot."

To see what would happen, he lightly touched some bread. At once it changed to gold.

"I do not see," he thought to himself, "how I am to eat any breakfast. Maybe if I move very fast I can do it."

He put a bite of egg into his mouth. He tried to swallow quickly. But the Golden Touch was too fast for him. He found his mouth full of hard gold. He cried out. Mary ran to him. Quickly she threw her arms around him.

"My sweet Mary," he said.

But Mary did not answer. She could not.

One minute she was a pretty little girl. The next she was gold. Midas covered his face with his hands. How long he sat this way, he did not know. Then he heard a voice saying:

"Hello, Midas. Tell me, are you enjoying the Golden Touch?"

The stranger was back — the god who had given him his terrible wish.

Midas shook his head. "I am very sad," he said.

"Very sad? How is that?" asked the stranger. "Didn't I keep my promise? Don't you have what you wanted to make you happy?"

"Oh, I was wrong. Gold is not everything," answered Midas.

"Do you really mean that, Midas? Which is worth more to you — the Golden Touch or a cup of water?"

"Oh, the water — the water!" said Midas. "If I could have just one drink."

"The Golden Touch," said the stranger, "or a piece of bread?"

"A piece of bread is worth all the gold on earth," answered Midas.

"The Golden Touch," asked the stranger, "or your own daughter Mary, as she was this morning?"

"I wouldn't give Mary up for the power to change the whole world to gold," cried Midas.

"You are a much wiser man than you were, King Midas," said the stranger. He looked hard at Midas. Then he said, "Tell me, do you really wish to lose the Golden Touch?"

"I hate it!" cried Midas.

"Then go to the river in your garden. Walk out into it. Take a large cup with you. Fill it with the river water. Sprinkle it over anything you wish to change back as it was."

King Midas bowed his head. When he lifted it, the stranger was gone. He ran as fast as he could to the river. He jumped into the water. As it covered him, the Golden Touch was washed away. He felt a change in himself. A cold, hard weight seemed to leave him. He hurried out with the cup of water. Seeing a pretty blue flower on the bank, Midas touched it. It stayed the same. Midas smiled.

He hurried back to the palace carrying the water. He sprinkled it on the golden Mary. As soon as it touched her, she was alive again. Together they went to the garden. There Midas sprinkled each of the golden flowers. They, too, became as they had been. The terrible Golden Touch was gone.

King Midas learned his lesson well. He lived to be an old man. But the only gold he loved was the gold in Mary's hair.

The
WONDERFUL
PITCHER

Jupiter, king of the gods, wanted a change from his life on Mt. Olympus. He sent for Mercury. Together they went down to earth.

"Mercury, we must look like other people," said Jupiter. "Take off your winged shoes and hat. Let's dress like travelers. We will have no adventures if people know who we are."

As it began to get dark, Jupiter and Mercury came to a village.

"We must find a place to stay," said Jupiter. "I'm getting hungry. Here's a house. Knock on the door."

Mercury knocked. A man opened it.

"What do you want?" he said.

"We are travelers. Will you give us something to eat and a place to sleep? We will pay you."

"We have no room for strangers." And the man closed the door with a bang.

Jupiter was angry.

"There was room for us! It was a big house. They are not very kind to people here. We'll have to go on, Mercury."

They went to the next house — and the next. Always it was the same. There was no room for strangers. There was not even a smile or a kind word.

"We are at the end of the town," said Mercury. "I can see only one more light. But the light is so dim, it can't be a house."

"Let's find out," said Jupiter.

The light was coming from a house — a very small house. As they came close they heard voices.

"Are you all right, my wife? I am sorry I was gone so long. No one will help us. They think only of themselves."

A woman's voice answered. "I am all right. Do not worry about the food. We have enough."

The gods looked at one another. Then Mercury knocked on the door. It opened at once. An old man stood there.

"Come in," he said. "Come in. Welcome to our home." And he opened the door wide.

"We are travelers," said Jupiter. "We need a place to sleep and something to eat."

"We are poor," said the old man. "We do not have much. But we will be glad to share what we have. My name is Philemon and this is my wife, Baucis."

Baucis brought vegetables from the garden to make a stew. She filled a pitcher with wine. Philemon set the table.

"Come, my friends," he said. "Sit down and eat. This is all we have. We wish it were more."

The food tasted good. The gods passed their glasses for more wine. The pitcher was not very big. Yet it was always full.

"Why should that be?" the old man wondered.

He looked at the strangers. They were smiling. Suddenly he knew.

"Wife!" he whispered. "These men are gods!"

They fell to their knees. "Forgive us. Our poor food is not good enough for gods. We did not know who you were."

"You gave us the best you had," said Jupiter kindly. "That was more than anyone else did. You shall have a reward for your kindness."

The next morning the old man and his wife went with the gods. They climbed a near-by hill. When they reached the top Jupiter said, "Look back."

The village was gone. In its place was a blue lake. The only house left was their own little hut.

Mercury pointed to it.

"Only your house was saved. The other people have been punished. And now you shall have your reward. What is your wish? Remember you may have what you wish."

117

The old people whispered to each other. Then Philemon, the old man, spoke.

"Our wish is a small one. We wish that we may always be together."

Mercury and Jupiter smiled. They were glad to give them their wish. They did even more. They changed the tiny house into a beautiful church.

The gods kept their promise. The old man and woman stayed together. When they died they became beautiful trees. Side by side they stood — still together.

The GREEKS *who* LEARNED *to* FLY

The Greeks knew nothing about airplanes. But they told a story about two men who learned to fly. Instead of an airplane they used wings as the birds do. This is their story.

Daedalus was a fine workman. He was very good at using all kinds of tools. He made many things for his king. But the king once grew angry with Daedalus. He ordered everything Daedalus owned sent to a far-off island. There Daedalus, his things, and his young son Icarus were locked in a tower.

It was easy for Daedalus to get out of the tower. He just used his tools to open the locks. The tower was on an island. Tools did not help much in getting off an island. Ships sailed from the island. But there was no way to escape on them. The king's men had orders to watch for Daedalus and his son.

"There must be some way we can get away," said Icarus to Daedalus. "You got us out of the tower, Father. Can't you think of a way to get us off this island?"

Daedalus tried many plans to get free. None of them worked. Then one day Icarus saw his father running toward him.

"This time I think I have it!" shouted Daedalus. "The king rules the land and sea, but he doesn't rule the air. The air is free. Why can't we try to escape through the air?"

"What are you talking about, Father?" said the boy. "How can we get away through the air? We can't fly like birds. That's a silly idea."

"Not so silly as you think," answered his father. "I think we can do it. Let's start right now. We'll need feathers. That's your job. Go out and gather all the feathers you can find. I want all kinds. Bring every feather you see, big or small. We can use them all."

Icarus still thought his father's idea was foolish, but did as he was told. He knew Daedalus was a very wise man. Maybe there was something to what he said.

"Anyway," he thought, "I haven't anything else to do. I might just as well be gathering feathers as sitting here doing nothing."

For days the boy gathered feathers. When he had enough of them, he went to his father.

"I have done as you said, Father. Here are the feathers. Now what do we do?"

"Now we are ready to begin. We will make the feathers into wings. We will use wax to hold the small feathers together. The large ones I'll sew on with thread. Let's start with the small feathers."

The boy and his father worked every day. Sometimes the wind blew the feathers away. Then the boy ran after them. At last the day came when the wings were finished. There were a pair for the boy and a pair for his father.

"They look just like the wings of giant birds, Father. Do you really think they will hold us? Will they carry us through the air? I can hardly wait to try."

"I'll try them first, Icarus. You stay here and watch."

Carefully Daedalus fastened the wings on his shoulders. He climbed a small hill near by. Then slowly moving his arms back and forth, he stepped into the air.

"They work, Father! They work!" shouted Icarus. "You are flying just like a bird. May I try now?"

Daedalus could hardly believe it. He could fly! No man had ever done it before. He climbed the hill again. Again he stepped into the air. Slowly he floated along. He found that he could go higher. All he had to do was move the wings faster.

"This is just the beginning, Son," he said when he landed. "We must learn how to stay in the air. It is a long way over the sea to our home. We will fly a little each day. When we are ready we can start the long trip."

Each day the boy and his father put on their wings. Each day they flew a little farther. At last they were ready for the long trip home.

"I think we can start now, Son," said Daedalus. "Come, I will fasten your wings for you."

He fastened the wings carefully. His hands shook when he tightened the straps. Tears ran down his face as he kissed the boy.

"Icarus, we are taking a terrible chance. If we fail we will fall into the sea and drown. Do not fly too low. The waters will make the feathers damp. If you fly too high the sun will melt the wax on your wings. Stay close to me, Son. May the gods watch over us!"

Saying this, Daedalus spread his wings and took off. Icarus followed him. As they flew over the island, people saw them.

"Are those birds?" they asked one another. "No, they can't be. They are too big for birds. They must be gods." They rubbed their eyes and shook their heads in wonder.

Daedalus and Icarus soon reached the sea. Daedalus turned around to look at his son. The boy was flying right behind him.

"Won't the king be surprised!" Daedalus thought. "Wait until he hears how we got away."

Again he turned around to look at Icarus. This time he could not see the boy. He was no longer behind him. Daedalus was frightened. Then he looked up. There was Icarus climbing higher in the sky.

"Come down, Icarus! Come down! You are too high. The hot sun will melt the wax on your wings. The feathers will come off. You will fall! Come down!"

He turned to fly back to the boy, but it was too late. The sun was already melting the wax. The feathers on Icarus' wings fell off one by one. The boy moved his wings as fast as he could. It did no good at all.

The wings would no longer hold him up.

"Help, Father!" he cried. "Come help me! I am falling."

Daedalus flew as fast as he could. But before he could get there, Icarus had fallen into the sea. All his father could see were a few feathers floating on the water.

Daedalus flew down closer. The boy was gone. He flew sadly on. All the joy of flying was gone. When he got home he put the wings in the temple of the gods. He never flew again.

ULYSSES

The Greeks had a war with some people called the Trojans. One of the leaders of the Greek soldiers was a man named Ulysses. Ulysses was a great Greek hero. The Greeks told many stories about him and his brave deeds.

Some of his most wonderful adventures happened right after the Trojan War. The Greeks wanted to get back home. So did Ulysses.

Soon after their ships left Troy, there was a terrible storm. The wind blew them to shore. They landed to find out where they were. The people of the country seemed glad to see them. They gave the soldiers food. Ulysses was not hungry and did not eat. It was good that he did not, for the food was magic food. Anyone who ate it forgot all about his home. One bite of this food and he wanted to stay in this country forever. All of Ulysses' men ate the magic food. Ulysses had to drag them back to the ship. He was happy to sail away from that land.

Their next adventure was in the land of the Cyclops. The Cyclops were giants. Their name means "round eye." They were called Cyclops because they had only one eye. It was a big, ugly eye, right in the middle of the forehead.

Ulysses and his men landed on the Cyclops' shore.

"Maybe we can get them to sell us food," said Ulysses. "We must have food and water before we can go on. We'll take this bottle of wine as a gift for them."

They found a large cave near the shore. Inside it were foods of all kinds.

"Surely this man will sell us something. He has more food than he needs. We'll sit down and wait for the owner to come."

They had not long to wait. Ulysses was frightened when he saw the Cyclops. The giant was at least nine feet tall. In the center of his forehead was one round eye.

The cave was so dark that the Cyclops did not see Ulysses and his men right away. He drove his sheep and goats into the cave. Then he rolled a large rock against the door of the cave. By this time his eye was used to the dark. Looking around he saw Ulysses and his men.

"Who are you?" he roared. "What are you doing in my cave?"

"We are Greek soldiers. We are going home from war. The wind blew our ship off its course. We need food. You have so much here. Will you sell us some?"

The Cyclops said not a word. Reaching out his long arms he grabbed two men. He threw them against the wall and killed them. Then he ate them. After this he lay down on the floor to sleep.

Ulysses spoke to his men when the Cyclops was asleep.

"Unless we can think of a plan," he said, "we will all die. Killing him now will do no good. We cannot move the stone from the door. Can any of you think of something we might do?"

They sat the rest of the night talking quietly. They tried to make some plans.

The next morning the giant killed and ate two more men. After this he moved the rock from the door. Then he led his animals out. Carefully he rolled the rock back into place. Ulysses and his men were alone in the cave.

"See that long stick over there?" said Ulysses. "We will work today to put a sharp point on it. When it is ready, we will hide it under the straw. Then we will wait for the giant to return."

In the evening, the Cyclops came back. As before, he drove in his animals and closed the door with the rock. Then he ate two more of Ulysses' men for his supper. When he had finished, Ulysses walked up to him. In his hands was the wine they had brought from the ship.

"Here is some wine, Cyclops. It is very good. Drink some if you like."

The giant took it and drank it all.

"That was good," he said. "Just for that I promise not to eat you until last. What is your name?"

"My name is No-man," answered Ulysses quickly.

"Well, No-man, I say good night. Your wine has made me sleepy."

Ulysses waited until he was sure the Cyclops was asleep. Then he whispered to his men, "Bring out the stick!"

Holding it over the fire, they heated the point. Then they stuck it deep into the giant's one eye.

He jumped up screaming, "My eye! My eye! I can't see! Help me!"

The other Cyclops heard him. From out side the cave they called, "What is wrong? Who is hurting you?"

"No-man is hurting me. He has made me blind!"

"Then we can't help you," said his friends. "If no man is hurting you, it must be the work of the gods. We don't dare help you if the gods are punishing you." And they went away.

In the morning the giant rolled away the rock. He had to let his sheep out to get some grass. He did not want the men to get out. So he felt each animal that passed him. The wise Ulysses thought the giant would do this. He found narrow strips of leather in the cave. With them he tied his men under the sheep. He tied three sheep together. Under the middle sheep was a man. The giant did not think of feeling under the sheep. So the Greeks all got out safely. They took the sheep with them on their boat. Then they left the island as fast as they could.

They had one more exciting adventure before they got home. One day they came to an island. Ulysses sent some men to shore in one of the small boats.

"See what country this is," he said. "Then we can tell how far we are from home."

The first thing on the island that the

men saw was a beautiful palace. As they came near it a young woman came out to meet them.

"My name is Circe," she said. "Welcome to my palace. Won't you come in?"

All the men but the captain followed her. He did not know why, but he did not trust this strange woman. He saw the men sit down to eat. The table was filled with the finest foods. The men were hungry. Circe went from one man to another.

"It has been a long time since you have eaten well," she said. "Eat as much as you wish. There is plenty here."

The men ate and ate. When they could eat no more, Circe got up. She touched each man on the shoulder. As she touched them, they turned into pigs. She then led them to a pig pen and closed the gates.

The captain watching outside saw this. He ran as fast as he could to the little boat. He rowed quickly out to the ship.

"Ulysses! Ulysses!" he cried. "Something terrible has happened!" And he told Ulysses what he had seen.

Ulysses did not know what to do. "I am only a soldier," he said. "I don't know anything about magic. What can I do to save my men?"

"It seems to me you need my help now, Ulysses," said a voice behind him. Ulysses turned around. There stood Mercury!

Mercury held out a small green plant. "Take this with you when you go to see Circe. When she isn't looking, crush the plant. Sprinkle it over the food she gives you. Do not eat anything not sprinkled with the plant. Then Circe can do nothing to you. When she cannot turn you into a pig, she will be frightened. Then it will be up to you to get her to do what you want."

Things happened just as Mercury said they would. Circe came out to meet Ulysses as she had met his men. After Ulysses ate, she touched his shoulder. But Ulysses had done as Mercury told him. When Circe touched him, nothing happened. He jumped up with his sword in his hand. "You cannot change me into a pig, Circe. And I will kill you if you do not do what

I say! Give all of my men back to me!"

Circe was frightened. "Do not kill me! I will give you your men."

She hurried to the pig pen. There she changed each pig into a man again. Circe could not understand why her magic had not worked on Ulysses.

"He must be a great man," she thought.

Before the Greeks left, she took him aside.

"Not far from here," she told him, "your ship will pass some women. They sit on rocks in the ocean and sing sweet songs. Any man who listens to them jumps into the water. He is never seen again. Make your plans, Ulysses, and be careful!"

Ulysses thanked Circe and said good-bye. Before they sailed, he put wax into his ears and into the ears of his men. They saw the singing women but could not hear them. So they went safely by.

"We have Circe to thank for saving us from those women and Mercury to thank for saving us from Circe," said Ulysses.

So after many a long day of sailing, they came at last to Greece.

Pronouncing Helps

Apollo (a-POLL-o), *god of the sun*

Arcas (AR-kus), *son of Callisto*

Argonauts (AR-go-nots), *men who sailed with Jason*

Argus (AR-gus), *man with a hundred eyes*

Atalanta (at-a-LAN-ta), *girl who could outrun a man*

Atlas (AT-lus), *giant holding up the world*

Baucis (BO-sis), *wife of Philemon*

Bellerophon (bel-LAIR-o-fon), *rider of Pegasus, the winged horse*

Callisto (ka-LIS-to), *woman turned into a bear*

Centaur (SEN-tor), *half man and half horse*

Ceres (SEE-reez), *goddess of the harvests*

Chiron (KY-ron), *centaur who was a great teacher*

Circe (SIR-see), *woman who turned Ulysses' men into pigs*

Cyclops (SY-klops), *giant with one eye*

Daedalus (DED-a-lus), *man who learned to fly*

Epimetheus (ep-i-ME-thoos), *brother of Prometheus and husband of Pandora*

Gorgons (GOR-guns), *Medusa and her two sisters*

Hercules (HER-kew-leez), *hero who freed Prometheus*

Hesperides (hes-PAIR-i-deez), *girls guarding the golden apples*

Icarus (IK-a-rus), *son of Daedalus*

Io (EYE-o), *girl turned into a white cow*

Juno (JOO-no), *queen of the gods*

Jupiter (JOO-pi-ter), *king of the gods*

Lycia (LISH-ee-a), *land where Bellerophon lived*

Medea (me-DEE-a), *helper of Jason in getting the Golden Fleece; later his wife*

Medusa (me-DOO-sa), *Gorgon with hair of snakes*

Mercury (MER-kew-ree), *messenger of the gods*

Midas (MY-das), *king whose touch turned all things to gold*

Minerva (mi-NUR-va), *goddess of wisdom*

Neptune (NEP-toon), *god of the sea*

Olympus (o-LIM-pus), *mountain home of the gods*

Pandora (pan-DO-ra), *young girl who brought troubles to Earth*

Pegasus (PEG-a-sus), *winged horse*

Perseus (PER-soos), *killer of Medusa*

Phaeton (FAY-e-ton), *boy who drove the sun*

Philemon (fi-LEE-mon), *old man turned into a tree*

Pluto (PLOO-to), *god of the underworld*

Prometheus, (pro-MEE-thoos), *god who brought fire to men*

Proserpine (pro-SUR-pee-nee), *daughter of Ceres, stolen by Pluto*

Ulysses (you-LIS-eez), *Greek soldier*

Venus (VEE-nus), *goddess of beauty*

Vulcan (VUL-kan), *god of fire, blacksmith of the gods*